Thoughts on Life and Faith

by

Trish Kelly

Copyright ©2016 Trish Kelly

ISBN: 978-1-326-72664-5

All rights reserved, including the right to reproduce this book, or portions thereof in any form. No part of this text may be reproduced, transmitted, downloaded, decompiled, reverse engineered or stored in any form or introduced into any information storage and retrieval system, in any form or by any means, whether electronic or mechanical without the express written permission of the author.

Published by

LODGE BOOKS

25 South Back Lane
Bridlington
www.lodgebooks.co.uk

Contents

Life's Not Fair	1
Jigsaws	3
Concert	5
Children cutting their hair/cooking	7
When the Oceans Rise and Thunders Roar	9
Rain Garden	12
Children of Israel	14
Knitting	16
What Is It Really Like In The Lion's Den?	18
Beer Goggles	19
Direction	20
Simon Says	21
Count Your Blessings	22
The Joy Of The Lord	23
From Fear To Victory	24
Mindblowing	25
Love	26
The Written Word	27
Reclamation	28
What Diet Are You On?	29
By His Stripes	31
Burning	32

Danger	33
Sharp Stones	34
Where Were You?	35
Gardening	36
Peace	37
Which Shoes Are You Wearing?	40
Which Label Are You Wearing?	41
Crossword Puzzles	42
Walk A Mile In My Shoes	43
Apprenticeships	44

Life's Not Fair

From a very young age we all discover how unfair life is.

As children we have to tidy our rooms, go to bed when we are told, eat our vegetables and many other things.

We also get blamed for things that our friends/siblings do.

As we grow up things don't change.

When we go out to work things are the same there. Colleagues blame us for things we didn't do, we get passed up for promotion.

It is easy to stamp our feet and say life isn't fair. The test is how we deal with these things. Jesus is still in charge of the situation and we should seek to see what he has planned for us.

Imagine how Jesus felt.

He was betrayed by his friends and crucified. He came into the world in human form to save the world. Instead of thanking him and following him, they let him down big time.

Jesus still carried on his journey, fulfilling what was expected of him

It would have been easier not to sacrifice himself in the way he did and blame the behaviour of mankind for his decision.

Instead, he was obedient to his father even to death on a cross.

When we are in an unfair situation, we should behave in the same way Jesus would.

Jigsaws

For those of you that do jigsaws, you will understand that there are different techniques to doing a jigsaw. First of all, there is no point in doing the jigsaw if there are pieces missing.

There is a school of thought that you put the outside pieces together first, then you group the various parts of the jigsaw, the people, animals, etc. Last of all you put in the sky or foliage.

The sky and the foliage are the hardest parts and all of the bits look the same. It takes a lot of time to do these bits.

We can put the pieces in a place where they don't belong and force them in. This just means that the correct piece will be left over and the jigsaw won't look right.

Likewise with a crossword puzzle. If we think we know the answer to a clue and put it in and it is wrong it throws the whole puzzle out. As we gain in knowledge we are less likely to make this mistake.

Watching a scary movie that we have seen before. We know the ending, but we still feel a sense of tension and anticipation when we watch the film for a second time. We should trust that we know the ending.

The point here is that when we try to manipulate things in our lives to make them work, like forcing the wrong jigsaw piece in place or filling in the wrong answer to a clue on a crossword puzzle we probably won't get things right. It is better by far to let God have the lead in things and guide us where we need to be. That way things work out perfectly.

Also throughout life we go through tough experiences. If we are wise, we will allow God to move in the situations and bring us through. Very often, once these situations are passed we forget what God has done. When another tough situation comes up we revert to doubting him and not believing he can bring us through. Instead, we should allow these situations to build our faith and remember what he has done for us and what he has brought us through.

Concert

We have been lucky enough to attend lots of concerts. There is the usual build up to any concert. You hear a certain group is coming to town and you get the dates/times.

You then wait for the tickets to come up for sale. Some people buy tickets ahead of them going on public sale, others queue up for hours or go online for hours to buy them.

Then, once you have got your tickets there is the long wait until the date of the concert.

At last the day arrives.

You plan your day so that you will arrive at the venue in good time. You get to the venue, find your seat and wait.

You have spent, usually, weeks leading up to this moment. Finally, the band comes on to the stage and it is all worthwhile.

Most concerts we have been to have begun on time and gone without a hitch.

It occurred to me at these concerts what it would be like if we were going to meet Jesus instead of seeing a band.

Do we put in the same effort and are we as excited at the prospect of an eternity in the presence of Jesus as we are at the prospect of an hour and a half in the presence of a band? We pay lots of money to see a band and go to great efforts; are we the same in our Christian journey?

One of the concerts was almost two hours late in starting. Nobody got up and went home. Everyone sat there patiently, eagerly awaiting the arrival of the band. Nobody seemed to be complaining. How many people give up and walk away from what God has in store for us? Do we wait patiently, excitedly, knowing what is ahead?

Children cutting their hair/cooking

Most of us know of a child that has attempted to cut their own hair. Some of us will know a child who has attempted to make mum breakfast in bed and left the kitchen looking like a bombsite.

At the time, we wish they hadn't bothered because it takes more to clean up than to have made the meal in the first place.

It would be easier and safer to have taken them to the hairdresser and got the job done properly.

It is funny how this compares to our prayer life.

So often we say "all I can do is pray". It sounds as if it is the least helpful thing we can do, a small offering in the midst of a big problem.

I believe God wants us to bring all things to him.

Children get in to worse scrapes than making a mess of their hair by cutting it themselves or making a mess of the kitchen when they are making something to eat. As parents we would prefer they came to us first rather than trying to sort things out for themselves. Nevertheless, when they have made a mess of sorting out a situation we still come to their rescue and see them through. We help them to learn from that particular situation.

So it is with God. He would like us to come to him first. To pray first instead of trying to use our own strength and thought process to get through. However, if we don't, he doesn't turn his back on his. He brings us through the situation and out the other side.

I have found myself many times saying to God "I can't do this, get me out of it". God doesn't necessarily seek to do that. He will, however, take us through the situation and help us emerge the other end stronger and wiser.

When the Oceans Rise and Thunders Roar

> *"When the oceans rise and thunders roar*
> *I will soar with you above the storm*
> *Jesus you are Lord over the flood*
> *I will be still, know you are God"*
>
> **(Taken from a song by Hillsong Church.)**

These are such lovely words.

Friends of ours were caught up in the Boxing Day Tsunami of 2004. Fortunately they were in the Maldives which is very flat and had little in the way of debris resulting from the tsunami.

Jan hadn't long learned to swim so when they were stood on the deck of their beach hut and the water began rising up through it, she was scared. Soon the word went out that they should evacuate to higher ground. The thing is there wasn't much higher ground.

I don't know too many details of what exactly happened; they don't say very much. Andy did say that if you need something to help you float, don't pick plastic furniture, it sinks!!

They survived to see another day, but the memory will always be there.

For us in our day to day lives we all have times when the oceans rise and the thunder roars. These are moments when we are out of our own strength and scared. For others looking on it may not seem that bad, but for us the fear is very real.

Imagine being on a small island, the water starts to rise up around you. There is nowhere to go. All of a sudden the thunder starts crashing around you. You are deafened by the noise, you cover your ears, but still it sounds. By now, the water is around your waist. You look around, there is nothing but sea all around you. What do you do? You know that even if you were the best swimmer in the world, where would you go? Which direction would you swim in? Chances are you would be swept off course anyway. There is no land in sight, so you probably wouldn't have the strength to get to land in any case.

Then, as you are accepting that you can't do anything, you pray.

In these situations we often hear people say "all I could do was pray". This should be our first option, not the option we turn to when we have exhausted our own resources.

At that point Jesus appears and carries you above the sea, above the clouds and thunder where the air is calm. What a relief.

Oceans rising and thunder roaring can come in many disguises: a bad day at work, the children making more noise than usual, financial worries, relationship issues, any day to day issue that we face that seeks to overwhelm us.

The bible says "Be still and know that I am God". How difficult to be still when you have water rising around your waist and the deafening sound of thunder all around you.

There is a picture painted by someone who was trying to describe what peace is like. It is of someone in the eye of a storm. The storm is raging all around and he is in the middle with Jesus.

As Christians we believe that God is Lord of everything. Yet, when we are in a situation that we cannot deal with we lose sight of that. We look at what we can do in our strength and when that fails we panic. It is when we are at the end of our own strength that God can demonstrate his power best. When we surrender to him, we can see what he can do and we can "be still and know that he is God".

Rain Garden

An issue arose during the building of our new home. We had to have something called a rain garden as a sort of holding tank for storm water to stop the mains drainage being inundated during storms.

This rain garden was an eyesore. It was awful at the time. It caused a lot of stress for both of us. We couldn't see a way through it.

A friend of ours came with me to a site meeting with the drain-layer and the builder to attempt to resolve matters. This did to a certain extent, but there was still the question that we were over budget and not sure how to make this up.

I stressed for a day or so and then prayed (I know, this was the wrong way around).

Anyway, once I prayed I felt peaceful as though it was going to be OK.

My husband went off to his men's group on the Friday morning. When he came home, he said that he had thought about what to do. He believed we should walk away from the situation and allow it to be what it would be. We should speak to the builder and explain that we needed to make up the overspend somewhere else on the build. He explained that he believed that this would maintain the good relationship we had with our builder and stop us getting bogged down in the situation. He said he had prayed about things and that is how he felt.

This was very different for my husband. He was calm, he spoke to me instead of at me and I was able to accept what he was saying. This was a real answer.

Children of Israel

When we pray for something, we should believe that God will answer. He will answer, although not maybe in a way we would like. Dr Schuler Snr of the Crystal Cathedral summed it up well. God answers prayer in one of three ways: "No" – meaning this is not in his plan for that situation; "Slow – meaning not at the moment, but some time in the future; and "Go" – meaning yes, now.

It is difficult with just our human understanding to accept the way God answers our prayers if it is not with the word "Go". When we become Christians we agree to follow Jesus wherever he leads us. Not with conditions.

The children of Israel are a good example of this.

They walked through the desert for forty years to get to where they needed to be and claim God's inheritance. This journey was a lifetime for most people.

On the journey people were born, married, died – all of life's events happened along the way. This is enough to make anyone give up, but they didn't. Many of the people who started the journey would not live to see the end. Some who finished the journey didn't see the beginning. This didn't stop them pressing on towards what God had for them, their promised land.

We should look at life like this. Many people say "life is not a rehearsal". There are other sayings that people use as an excuse to play hard and fast. It is true, we only have one life and we should make the most of it. This doesn't mean living fast and disobeying what God has asked us to do and not living the way he wants us to. We should aim to do what is right and store up "treasures in Heaven". We will spend so much more time in eternity than we do on earth.

Knitting

I apologise for those people here who are not knitters. For people who knit a display of knitting wool is beautiful. All the different colours and textures. The knitting patterns which show us what we can turn these wonderful yarns into.

When you knit something it is important to make sure that you use the right size knitting needles as different size needles will create different knitting. We are all like strands of wool of different colours and different textures.

When wool is knitted up into a jumper or another item, the wool is mixed together to make something beautiful. If you unpick the item, the wool is no longer straight and shiny, it is all crinkled. Scraps of wool look scruffy and old. The wool might have become tangled and need the tangles cut out so that there may not be enough wool for a jumper. Then you will need to tie bits together to have enough to knit an item. Once again the scruffy bits of wool can join together to make something beautiful again.

This is how life can be. When we are born we are brand new. Over time we join with others to make something new, when we are married we have joined with someone else to make a couple, we have children and create a family, we join with other Christians and make a church, we join with friends.

Then, as we go through life we can become unravelled through life's problems. It doesn't have to end here. We need to understand that through God's grace we can be joined with others to make something beautiful again.

What Is It Really Like In The Lion's Den?

Shadrach, Meshack and Abednigo / Daniel in the Lion's Den / David and Goliath.

None of these are believable in today's world.

This doesn't mean that these stories don't relate to us in today's world.

Our situations are very often similar, we may feel like we are in a fiery furnace, in a lion's den or up against a wall.

God is still relevant in these situations and can still bring us through them, very often stronger than we were before. These situations form part of our ongoing testimony and, if we are wise, can help others who face similar situations in the future.

Beer Goggles

You have heard of the sayings "beer goggles" and "through rose coloured glasses".

How about faith goggles? We could say that this is looking at our situation the way Jesus would have. We look at things with faith that God can move.

We should look at life with "faith goggles". This shows us that all things are possible.

Direction

A mother takes her child to the shops.

The child thinks he will be getting some sweets when visiting the sweet shop.

They get to the shop, but mum has other ideas.

This is much the same how things are with us. We make all sorts of plans for ourselves, but God has other ideas. He has a perfect plan for our lives.

We have intentions and plans, but God directs our steps.

Simon Says

Imagine that your Vicar stands up on Sunday and says, "I believe it would be good to do a sponsored parachute jump for charity. Can we have a show of hands?"

How would everyone react? How many would immediately sign up? Not many. This is just someone's random crazy idea.

When we are in a difficult situation and someone gives us advice, we should consider if their advice is the best for us or whether it is just their own personal opinion on what we should do. Their advice comes from their own experiences and may not be the best for us.

Likewise, in our Christian walk, we should test the spirits so that we know if it is God. Just because a fellow Christian suggests something, it doesn't make it right.

Just like Simon Says.

Count Your Blessings

"Count Your Blessings." How many times have we heard this?

It seems an easy thing to do until you are in the middle of a storm. When we are facing life's difficulties, the last thing we want to do is count our blessings – most of the time we can't even see our blessings.

However, if we are able to just think of a handful of positive things, it is a start:-

- We are alive in the world;
- We have clothes to wear / food to eat;
- We live in a country with freedom of speech.

If we try hard enough we can come up with many blessings. This begins a chain reaction – coming up with blessings becomes easier and easier. This leads to happiness inside, which leads to a joyful feeling and a different outlook on our original situation.

The Joy Of The Lord

"The Joy of the Lord is my Strength."

When we are in the middle of one of life's difficult situations it is so easy to feel all alone. We can often feel that we are the only person to have gone through that particular situation or to feel that particular emotion.

If we have good friends or family around us, they can encourage us and help us to feel stronger.

When a big disaster occurs, it often happens that the survivors form a group to support and encourage each other as they draw strength from one another.

If we were to draw near to God and view him as our father / friend we will gain much strength from that.

After all, he is greater than any friend or relative we have here on earth.

From Fear To Victory

To most of us the distance from fear to victory is so great and so daunting we can't see a way from one to the other.

There is a common theme amongst abused people – they are scared to speak out. With children, the abusers tell them it is their little secret or scare them into not speaking. With adults, it can be a pride thing. This is the same as Satan – he tricks us into believing we can't speak out and holds us in fear.

Victory comes in many ways. It is how we interpret it that counts.

We once faced a difficult and challenging time which proved costly.

The matter went to Court. We had lots of people praying for us and prepared our case well. We were confident that God would support us. The day came and although we did the right thing, we still lost the case.

This does not seem to be a victory. We lost the case, but won in other areas.

We were later applying for our superannuation from New Zealand. I was expecting a certain amount. This amount was increased by almost double. This gave us five hundred pounds above what we had to pay out. This is a victory.

We are told that God gives us "double for our trouble".

Mindblowing

Watching the 'Stargazing' programme, they had Buzz Aldren as one of their guests.

The interview was fascinating – just watching someone who had actually walked on the moon was brilliant.

For the fellow guests and the audience this was mindblowing.

Just pause for a moment to consider how mind-blowing it is that we are able to come into the presence of the God who created this universe.

Love

We are familiar with the chapter Corinthians 1, chapter 13 on love. How often do we really think about what the words mean?

Love trusts all, love believes all. Do we follow these words in our everyday life towards others?

There may be times when we feel that we are not being given the whole truth, if we confront the person it may cause more problems than it solves. It is better that we leave people to God to deal with and that we lift them up in prayer.

We can literally love someone into the kingdom by showing God's love to them.

The Written Word

We all know what it is like to wait on a letter. Perhaps a letter containing exam results or to confirm we have succeeded in getting a job. The wait seems to go on forever.

We tell ourselves that we will be OK no matter what the contents of the letter, but that is easier said than done.

I remember waiting for the letter to tell me my divorce had been finalised. I couldn't wait for it to arrive. It was a different thing altogether to see it in writing. The reality of what it all meant was very different.

Likewise, we receive the long awaited letter confirming we have succeeded in getting our dream job. The initial reaction is joy that we have been successful, closely followed by anxiety that we are up to the job.

It is the same with the Bible. Many of us will know certain passages of scripture off by heart. We will have read it many times and could quote it easily. However, there are times when we can read the same passage and the words jump right off the page at us. This is a word in season when we need it.

Reclamation

It is a great thing to see the difference in an item "before" and "after" it has been restored. Equally, it is encouraging to see the change in someone who has lost weight or had a makeover. The differences can be remarkable.

What was run down can become useful again. When we become Christians we are new creations.

This is the same for our country. I believe that we should pray for our country, that it becomes the best it can be.

What Diet Are You On?

A good diet, we are told, is very important. Eat the right things, drink the right things, exercise the right amount. There are such a variety of diets it is mind-blowing; which one is right for us?

Are we also concerned about what we are feeding on in our environment? An example of this is what we watch on TV.

One morning while I was doing my paperwork I had the TV on in the background. An announcement on the TV said that the next programme carried a PG rating as it was unsuitable for children. The programme was The Waltons. The programme after that also had a PG rating – that was Little House On The Prairie. These are two programmes that most of us grew up with as children.

That is not my only surprise with what appears on our TV screens. Some of the adverts that are shown contain more adult themes than The Waltons or Little House On The Prairie.

The question is – what sort of influence does this sort of censorship have on us? If we followed the TV schedule makers we would allow our children to watch suspect adverts portraying men in a feminine way, but not let them watch a programme like 'The Waltons' about a normal family working and supporting each other through the depression years and the war years. What about 'Little House On The Prairie' made by Michael

Landon who was a Christian and portrayed another normal family working together to survive hard times and portraying clearly Christian values in every episode.

Pray into this situation that the Holy Spirit will come into the situation and influence the people who create the TV schedules.

By His Stripes

There is a price to pay for every action. There are some children who seem to spend their time constantly in detention or in the Headmaster's Office. At one time this could involve being given the cane.

Adults who commit crimes also face consequences. A prison sentence and in some countries the death penalty.

Imagine if someone visited the person who had committed the crime and said they would endure the punishment on their behalf. Who wouldn't jump at the chance?

Yet, how many people that are offered the gospel turn away?

Jesus went to the cross on our behalf and took our sins upon his own shoulders.

By His Stripes We Are Healed

Burning

We have all burnt our hand. It could be on an iron, an oven door, hot water splashing from a saucepan. For a small burn the pain is huge. Instantly putting our hand under the cold tap will ease this pain.

We can remember being sunburned and getting into the shower, such pain.

Imagine having burns over 40% of your body, unbelievably painful.

The treatment is not as easy as to stand under a cold shower. In this case the skin has blistered and peeled off, leaving the flesh red raw and open to infection.

When such large areas are burned there is a need for skin grafts. This treatment in itself is no picnic, it is extremely painful and takes a long, long time.

Skin grafts are required over a long period of time until the area is healed. We tolerate such discomfort and pain because we know we will be made whole again.

Likewise with us, our sin can take up quite a large part of us and require ongoing healing until the wound is healed. It can be a long drawn out, painful process. It is then we should have our eye firmly on the goal ahead, peace in our heart and mind and the promise of eternal life.

Danger

It seems that children have a natural attraction towards dangerous things, they are likely to pull at a saucepan on a hob unit or put their hands near to a fire, both actions would result in awful burns.

When my children were young we had one of the old gas fires with the concrete bricks that lit up orange. I had a large fireguard that surrounded the fire. My daughter used to like to try and get close enough to put her fingers near the fire. I would move her away and tell her not to touch and explain that it would burn her. Still she seemed to get too close to the fire. I warned and warned her, but still she persisted.

Imagine if she had touched the fire with just one finger, how much pain that would cause. How much more pain if she had fallen onto it?

So it is with God. He sees us flirting with danger and warns us, attempts to teach us a different way to go about things. He just wants us to move forward without the need to get hurt in the process.

This can only be done if we are obedient to him and not try to do things our way.

Sharp Stones

We have all played at the seaside and found pieces of glass that have been in the sea for a long time.

What started off as jagged pieces of glass become smooth stone-like objects after their time in the sea.

It is just the same for us. We are a particular, unique shape and as God's love surrounds us, we are smoothed and honed into a new shape.

Where Were You?

We have all heard the phrase "I can remember where I was when ...... happened".

Or "I remember where I was when ...... died".

This is usually because a momentous event in history and the death of a celebrity is reported on every type of media.

Imagine the outpouring of grief at the death of a celebrity.

Now try and imagine if the reports of the celebrity's death had been a mistake. What relief the fans would feel. The feelings of loss turning into feelings of elation. The thought that they will be able to continue to make more films / music.

This is how it was with Jesus' followers. They witnessed him die on the cross and were grief-stricken. Then, after three days he rose again.

If we are elated when we discover that reports of a celebrity's death have been misreported, how excited we should feel to know that Jesus is alive.

Gardening

I am not a very good gardener, I just don't have green fingers.

For instance, the other day I was weeding and managed to pull out a clematis plant that my husband had planted and started to train around a trellis on the wall.

When I buy vegetable / fruit plants I always put the label next to them so that I know what is supposed to grow on them.

All plants and trees are distinguished by the type of leaves they have and / or the types of fruit / vegetables that grow on them.

The same is true for Christians; they will be known by their fruit.

When someone who does not know Jesus looks at us, they should see a difference in us, we should demonstrate the fruits of the spirits in our lives.

Peace

Peace is very subjective.

If you were to talk to several different people, they would all have a different idea of what peace is.

To the young mother with one or two small children, peace is being able to spend an hour on her own doing what she wants to.

To an office worker in a high-rise building it may be to get out of the office at lunchtime and walk in a park.

To someone who lives in a busy city, it is being able to get away to the country.

We all have our own ideas of peace.

Peace is usually associated with Quiet as in "Peace and Quiet" or Rest.

Everyone can achieve their desire for peace. We all have moments of peace within our lives otherwise we would go insane.

So it is easy to find those moments of peace and calm when the stress is over and the children are in bed, the work day is finished or the holiday time has arrived.

What about when we are back in those stressful situations – what then? How do people get through?

For Christians it is a bit different. We are able to experience the "peace that passes all understanding" *even* and *especially* during the tough times. This is an inner peace which helps us to remain calm through the storm and not just after it has passed. We are not rocked by the rollercoaster effect of the storm.

Rudyard Kipling wrote: "If you can keep your head when all around are losing theirs" and the last line "you'll be a man my son". I believe this means you will be mature.

Just as we talked about faith growing in adversity, our sense of peace becomes more precious and more prominent during difficult times.

Sometimes, when the storms of life rage around us, people who don't know God will look at us for an example. If we can show the fruit of peace in our lives and that we trust God it will be a real witness.

The prayer of St Francis for example says:

> *"Make me a channel of your peace."*

> and

> *"Where there is darkness, only light."*

We are to be salt and light into the world.

So peace is not just something we can achieve when we are in a quiet moment, it is something we trust God for during tough times. It is a time of quiet, rest and reflection to restore our souls. A time when we can connect with God in a closer way and hear his voice.

Which Shoes Are You Wearing?

Do you have an old pair of shoes that you just love? Maybe they are old and tatty, but you like them because they are comfortable.

You could buy a new pair, but they would take some time to wear in and hurt your feet at first.

So what do you do? Carry on with the old shoes and keep making repairs to them or do you buy the new ones and put up with the pain for a while?

Life is like this. We are usually stuck in certain behaviour. We may not like how our life is going, but it is what we know. It's our comfort zone. Just like the old shoes, not perfect, but familiar.

Or, we could reach out and change things for the better. This option comes with a little pain in the short-term, but will benefit us long-term and last longer, just like the new shoes.

Which Label Are You Wearing?

All of us have been through difficult life experiences. How we approach and react to these difficulties shapes our character going forward.

There are times when we take one hit after another after another and wonder if we will ever be able to get up, let alone stand – we can easily take on the role of victim.

If we get stuck into that mindset, we will approach the next situation in the same way.

This will most likely mean that people will see us that way and approach us as a victim. As the saying goes: "has the word victim written on his / her forehead."

If we make a conscious decision to change the way we view ourselves, others will view us differently.

So are you wearing a badge that says "Victim" or "Victor" today? It is your decision to make.

Crossword Puzzles

People that do crossword puzzles and competitions on a regular basis will tell you that once you get into the mindset of the person compiling the puzzles, they become easier. It is like learning a new language.

The same is true when you join a leisure class such as photography. When you first join the class you know very little. The people there seem to speak in their own language which has no meaning to you. As time goes on, you become familiar with this new language and in turn you will become more knowledgeable about the subject.

It is the same in our Christian walk. At the beginning we are surrounded by people who all seem to know what they are talking about and understand more than we do. As we move forward and spend time in their company, our understanding will increase.

Walk A Mile In My Shoes

How many of us have been to a friend's house and they get out the (seemingly endless) photos of their latest holiday? This can also be true of people who have just got a new puppy or had a new baby.

Whilst they are so enthusiastic about the photos, we can often find our thoughts drifting away to thoughts of what we will have for supper or running through our shopping list in our heads.

It is easy to forget that to them these photos represent something special.

It pays to stop and think how we feel about our pets / children / holiday photographs. We would want people to look at them and compliment us.

So it is with life experiences. We may not always be in the mood to listen to someone's problems or to provide the practical help that they need. It is at this time we should think about what it would be like if we were in such need, how we would feel if someone were there to offer the help we need.

We should be prepared to be a friend to those around us as much as we would like them to be a friend to us.

Apprenticeships

Have you noticed how a lot of the old trades are not practised so much now? There was a time when apprenticeships in carpentry, electrics, bricklaying and many other skills were widely available.

Many other old skills have been lost too, such as willow working and weaving. Such skills were often passed down through generations of the same family.

What skills and lessons in life are we passing on to the future generations of our family? What will be our legacy to them?